Everyone Gets Ready

by Joan Doyle
illustrated by Marsha Winborn

Scott Foresman
is an imprint of

Glenview, Illinois • Boston, Massachusetts • Mesa, Arizona
Shoreview, Minnesota • Upper Saddle River, New Jersey

Every effort has been made to secure permission and provide appropriate credit for photographic material. The publisher deeply regrets any omission and pledges to correct errors called to its attention in subsequent editions.

Unless otherwise acknowledged, all photographs are the property of Pearson.

Photo locations denoted as follows: Top (T), Center (C), Bottom (B), Left (L), Right (R), Background (Bkgd)

Illustrations by Marsha Winborn

Photograph 16 Corbis

ISBN 13: 978-0-328-39376-3
ISBN 10: 0-328-39376-2

1 2 3 4 5 6 7 8 9 10 V010 17 16 15 14 13 12 11 10 09 08

Characters

Narrator

Silver, the grey squirrel

Stripes, the chipmunk

Tess, the badger

Tiny, the field mouse

Scene I: Under the Great Oak Tree

Narrator: It is autumn. The days are growing shorter, and all the animals know that the cold winds of winter will soon be blowing. Silver, the squirrel, and Stripes, the chipmunk, have played together all summer. Now that winter is coming, Silver and Stripes have been working hard, looking for food to store. They have not seen each other for a long time, but one day they run into each other, under the Great Oak Tree.

(Silver runs on stage, up to Stripes who is looking around.)

Silver: Is that you, Stripes?

Stripes: Why yes, it is. Is that you, Silver?

Silver: Yes it is. What are you doing in my part of the woods today?

Stripes: I've been looking for nuts and seeds to store for the winter, but I haven't found enough. I thought I'd come to this part of the woods to gather up acorns that fall from the Great Oak Tree.

Silver: There aren't many nuts or seeds on this side of the forest either. The badgers and raccoons got most of the acorns from the Great Oak Tree.

Stripes: Well, I guess I'll look under other oak trees around here. There must be some acorns left.

(Stripes starts to search under a tree.)

Silver: No, Stripes! You must go back to your side of the woods. This side is for me! I don't want you taking all my nuts and seeds!

Stripes: Who said this was your side of the woods? We both played here together all summer long, and I thought we were friends!

Silver: Well, summer is over now. We can't be friends anymore. Now we need to find food for survival. Go away, Stripes!

(Stripes turns and starts to walk away.)

Scene II: The Crossroads

Narrator: So Stripes sadly walked away. He walked for a long time until he reached the crossroads between the two forests. Stripes had just sat down to rest when he heard a voice. It was Tiny, the field mouse.

Tiny: Hi, Stripes! What's wrong?

(Stripes turns his head to see Tiny.)

Stripes: I'm sad, Tiny.

Tiny: Why are you so sad?

Stripes: Silver said that we can't be friends anymore. Winter is coming and I don't have enough food, so I came to this side of the woods to look for more food. But Silver doesn't want me looking for nuts and seeds on his side of the forest.

Tiny: *His* side of the forest? Silver said this was his side of the forest? This isn't Silver's side, the forest belongs to all of us!

Stripes: But what about the nuts? And the berries? Who do those belong to?

Tiny: All the food in the forest belongs to all of us too. I live on the other side of the forest, but I came here to look for food to take to my family.

Stripes: Well . . . maybe you're right, but I don't think Silver sees it that way. If I look for seeds here, he'll be angry with me.

Tiny: I have an idea that I think will help. Let's go talk to Silver.

(Tiny and Stripes walk off together.)

Narrator: Tiny and Stripes walked along together looking for Silver. Along the way, they picked up a few seeds. Finally, they saw Silver, scurrying up a tree.

(Tiny and Stripes look up into the tree.)

Tiny: Hey, Silver. Will you come down and talk to us?

Silver: I'm too busy. I have been working all by myself to get enough food for my family for the winter.

Tiny: We have been working too, but we need to work together if any of us wants to have enough food for the winter.

Scene III: The Forest

(Silver comes down from the tree.)

Silver: We need to work together? I hadn't thought of that. How can we work together and each get what we need as well?

Stripes: We can make a partnership.

Tiny: What's a partnership?

Stripes: It means we work together to get more than we each could get alone. Then we divide what we have evenly . . . the same amount for each of us.

Silver: I get it! We gather a huge pile of nuts, seeds, pine cones, and tasty berries. Then we can each take an equal part and take that to our homes. We'll work faster if we work together!

Tiny: It's a great solution. It will be fun.

(All three run and look in different directions.)

Narrator: So the three friends set to work. They worked day and night, finding as much food as they could, but soon they noticed Tess, the badger, eating some of the food they had found.

(Tess walks over to the pile of food.)

Silver: Hey, Tess! What are you doing? That's our food!

Tess: I'm sorry. I am hungry and I saw a large pile of my favorite snacks just sitting here. How did you get so many seeds? Look at all those nuts! I can't find anything to eat.

Stripes: Silver, Tiny, and I decided to work as a team, in a partnership.

Narrator: Tess was sad, she could not find any food. Silver and Stripes did not want her to take theirs. They didn't know how to fix this problem.

(Tiny sees Tess, and runs over to the group.)

Tiny: Hi, Tess. What is going on here?

Silver: We cannot give Tess any of our food because then we would not have enough, but she is hungry too. What should we do?

Tiny: Well, hold on a minute! A true partnership works better if there are more members to help.

Silver: Really? Do you think we should ask Tess to join us?

Tiny: Yes. Tess needs food for the winter too, and then she would not have to take it.

Narrator: The four animals sat and thought about what Tiny had said.

(Tess jumps up in the air, excited.)

Tess: I've got it! If you let me join your partnership, I can help carry sticks and stones too. You can use them to make your homes warmer and stronger for the winter. I am bigger and can carry things you cannot.

All: That's true!

Stripes: Tess, you are very smart. What a great plan!

(The animals run off in different directions.)

Scene IV: Winter in the Woods

Narrator: So they all started working together and soon had a huge pile. But they did not have much time to be proud of their pile because they had worked for so long that they had not realized it was starting to snow!

Stripes: Look at all this food! Mrs. Stripes will be so happy.

(Tiny points to the sky. The animals look up.)

Tiny: Oh, wow! It is starting to snow!

Silver: Hurry! Let's take all of this home.

Tess: After we are done, you can all come to my house and share our first winter meal.

All: Yeah!

(The animals give each other high fives.)

Hibernation

Some animals that live in the forest gather food for the winter. They work during the fall to get as much food as they will need to eat. Then the animals eat a lot of this food at the beginning of winter. They try to get fat so they will be ready to hibernate.

Hibernating means that they go into a deep sleep for most of the winter. They eat so much of the food that they gathered in the fall, that they are not hungry when they are sleeping. They do not have to wake up for a long time! Some animals, such as bears, can sleep all the way until springtime.